Tapi, Abis, Pasair

or

But, So, Because

Buku 3

Book 3 - Conjunctions

Chakapan Baba Ni Ari series

Baba Malay Today series

All Rights Reserved.
No part of this publication may be reproduced, stored in a retrieval system, or transmitted, in any form or by any means electronic, mechanical, photocopying, recording or otherwise, without the prior written permission of the publishers.

Theresa Fuller asserts the moral right to be identified as the author of this work.

Bare Bear Media

ISBN 978-1-925748-18-5 - Print
ISBN 978-1-925748-19-2 - Ebook

Cover by Helzkat Designs

Copyright November 2022©

Sincere thanks to my husband, Paul, who supported this work in every way possible. I love you.

National Library of Australia
US Library of Congress - TXu 2-349-549

Published 2nd of January 2023

Introduction - Conjunctions

Language is powerful.

In writing this text, I applied the SHOW don't TELL method. I wanted the reader to be able to pick up this book and begin to learn. Much as you would pick up a game and play.

> Chobak.
>
> To try.

The next rules I wish to expound are these:

1. Subject + Verb + Object, + [Conjunction] + Subject + Verb + Object.

2. Subject + Verb + Object, + [Conjunction] + Object.

3. [Conjunction], + Subject + Verb + Object, + Subject + Verb + Object.

At the end of the day, have fun.

This is Baba Malay, the language of the Peranakans.

> **YOUR** language.

Baba Malay

Baba Malay is the language of my ancestors.

A language that I discovered late in 2021 was about to go extinct with fewer than a thousand speakers in the world. I took a course in Baba Malay taught by Kenneth Chan, author of *BABA MALAY FOR EVERYONE - A comprehensive guide to the Peranakan language*. This was my start to saving Baba Malay.

But I believed much more had to be done.

The book you hold in your hands is the result of my mad persistence to save my language. While there are books out there on Baba Malay, I found little in the way for children. As a teacher, I believe that to save a language we must start with the young.

I wanted a book that parents could give to their children.
One I could give to my kids.

This is my attempt.

Theresa, affectionately known in the Peranakan community as Bibek Theresa.

    Sydney,
    29th of May, 2022

Chobak

Chobak = To Try

I love Baba Malay.

Contents

Introduction	3
Baba Malay	4
Tapi - But	8
Ka - Or	10
Chobak - Tapi/Ka	12
Pasair - Because	14
Chobak - Tapi/Ka/Pasair	16
Kalu - If	18
Sunggupun - Although	19
Chobak Kalu/Sunggupun	20
Chobak Tapi/Ka/Pasair/Kalu/Sunggupun	21
Sama - With	22
Pasair Tu - So	23
Abis - So, Then, Therefore	24
Chobak Sama/Pasair Tu/Abis/Dan	25
Forms of Conjunctions in English	26
Notes	30
About the Author	31
More books in the Baba Malay Today Series	32

TAPI - But

Clothes = Baju

But = Tapi

We generally use conjunctions to connect clauses or sentences. **'BUT'** is generally used to connect two opposing ideas.

Sentence 1:	Gua mo beli baju. I want to buy clothes.
Sentence 2:	Gua tak'ah duit. I have no money.
Joined:	Gua mo beli baju, **TAPI** gua tak'ah duit. I want to buy clothes, **BUT** I have no money.
Sentence 1:	Dia mo belajair Chakapan Baba. She wants to learn Baba Malay.
Sentence 2:	Dia tak'ah buku. She has no book.
Joined:	Dia mo belajair Chakapan Baba, tapi tak'ah buku. She wants to learn Baba Malay, but has no book.

TAPI - But Continued

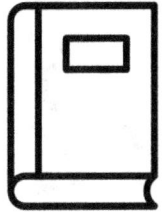

Book = Buku

Sentence 1:   Kita tak pi Malacca.
              We didn't go to Malacca.

Sentence 2:   Kita ada pi Penang.
              We did go to Penang.

Joined: Kita tak pi Malacca, tapi kita ada pi Penang.
              We didn't go to Malacca, but we did go to Penang.

Glossary
Ada = Have or Did
Baju = Clothes
Belajair = Study
Beli = Buy
Buku = Book
Chakapan Baba = Baba Malay
Dia = He/She   Dia Mia = His or Hers
Duit = Money
Gua = I   Gua Mia = My
Kita = We   Kita Mia = Our
Lu = You   Lu Mia = Your
Mo = Want
Pi = Go
Sapa = Who
Tak = Not
Tak'ah = Have no/ Do not have /There is not

KA - Or

Cake = Kueh

Or = Ka or Ato

In English, we generally use **'OR'** to show choices.

Sentence 1:   Lu mo makan kueh?
You want to eat cake?

Sentence 2:   Lu mo makan nasi?
You want to eat rice?

Joined: Lu mo makan nasi, **ATO** kueh?
Do you want to eat rice, **OR** cake?

Sentence 1:   Gua boleh pakay baju kebaya.
I can wear the baju kebaya.

Sentence 2:   Gua boleh pakay baju panjang.
I can wear the baju panjang.

Joined: Gua boleh pakay baju kebaya, **KA** baju panjang.
I can wear the baju kebaya, **OR** the baju panjang.

KA - Or Continued

Garden = Kebun

We can also use **'OR'** with questions.

Sentence: Jorang jalan ka, tak jalan?
            They are walking, or not?

Sentence: Dia belajair ka, tak belajair?
            Is she studying, or not studying?

Glossary
Anak-beranak = Family
Baju Kebaya = A short blouse worn with a sarong (worn by ladies)
Baju Panjang = 3/4 length Nonya dress worn with a sarong
Boleh = Can,   Tak Boleh = Cannot
Ini/Ni = This   Itu/Tu = That
Jalan = Walk
Jorang = They, Those People
Kueh = Cake
Makan = Eat
Main = Play   Main Kebun = Gardening
Mo = Want
Nasi = Rice
Pakay = Wear

CHOBAK - TAPI/KA/ATO

Sweater = Baju sweater

Select the correct word

I want to go buy a cake, but I have no money.
e.g. Gua mo beli kueh, (tapi/ka/ato) gua tak'ah duit.

1. I want to wear a sweater, but I do not have a sweater.
   Gua mo pakay baju sweater, (tapi/ka) gua tak'ah baju sweater.

2. I want to buy a book, or a cake.
   Gua mo beli buku, (tapi/ka) kueh.

3. I want to wear a sweater, or a jumper.
   Gua mo pakay baju sweater, (tapi/ka) baju jumper.

4. He wants to go for a walk, or a trip.
   Dia mo pi jalan, (tapi/ato) trip.

5. They want to buy books, but have no money.
   Jorang mo beli buku-buku, (tapi/ato) tak'ah duit.

Answers: 1. Tapi. 2. Ka. 3. Ka. 4. Ato. 5. Tapi.

CHOBAK - TAPI/KA/ATO

Cake = Kueh

Select the correct word

1. We bought a book, but did not buy a cake.
   Kita beli buku, (tapi/ka) tak beli kueh.

2. They did not garden or play.
   Jorang tak main kebun, (tapi/ato) main.

3. You all did not garden, but played.
   Lorang tak main kebun, (tapi/ka/ato) main.

4. Our family wanted to go to Malacca, but went to Penang.
   Kita mia anak-beranak mo pi Malacca, (tapi/ka/ato) pi Penang.

5. We want to go to Australia, or New Zealand.
   Kita mo pi Australia, (tapi/ka/ato) New Zealand.

6. Who is that? Is that your big sister, or your big brother?
   Sapa tu? Tu lu mia tachi, (tapi/ka/ato) lu mia hia?

Answers: 1. Tapi. 2. Ato. 3. Tapi. 4. Tapi. 5. Ka/Ato. 6. Ka/Ato.

PASAIR - Because

Bird = Burung

Because = Pasair, Sebab, Kerna.

To give the reason for. The word '**Pasair**' has many meanings. It can also mean '**market**' so always watch out for the context.

Sentence 1: Gua mo pi sana.
I want to go there.

Sentence 2: Gua mo tengok burung.
I want to see the birds.

Joined: Gua mo pi sana, **PASAIR** gua mo tengok burung.
I want to go to there, **BECAUSE** I want to see the birds.

Sentence 1: Lu mo pi Sydney.
You want to go to Sydney.

Sentence 2: Lu mo belajair.
You want to study.

Joined: Lu mo pi Sydney, pasair lu mo belajair.
You want to go to Sydney, because you want to study.

PASAIR - Because Continued

Ben

Sentence 1:   Ben mo bawak kereta.
              Ben wants to drive.

Sentence 2:   Ben mo pi kerja.
              Ben wants to go to work.

Joined: Ben mo bawak kereta, pasair dia mo pi kerja.
              Ben wants to drive, because he wants to go to work.

Glossary

Bawak Kereta = Drive
Belajair = Study
Kereta = Car
Kerja = Work
Lu = You
Mo = Want
Sana = There
Sini = Here
Tengok = See

CHOBAK - TAPI/KA/PASAIR

Big sister = Tachi

Select the correct word

1. Does your big sister, or big brother want to drive?
   Lu mia tachi, (tapi/ka/pasair) lu mia hia mo bawak kereta?

2. I will go to Australia, because I want to see my big sister.
   Gua mo pi Australia, (tapi/ka/pasair) gua mo tengok gua mia tachi.

3. They want to buy a cake, but they have no money.
   Jorang mo beli kueh, (tapi/ka/pasair) jorang tak'ah duit.

4. We want to eat rice, but not cake.
   Kita mo makan nasi, (tapi/ka/pasair) tak mo makan kueh.

5. My big brother wants a car, because he wants to drive.
   Gua mia hia mo kereta, (tapi/ka/pasair) dia mo bawak kereta.

6. Walk, or drive to school?
   Jalan, (tapi/ka/pasair) bawak kereta pi sekolah?

Answers: 1. Ka. 2. Pasair. 3. Tapi. 4. Tapi. 5. Pasair. 6. Ka.

CHOBAK - TAPI/KA/PASAIR

Big brother = Hia
Translate into Baba Malay

1. Your big brother, or big sister is coming.
2. Ben wants to drive, but he has no car.
3. I want to go to Australia, because I want to see kangaroos.
4. Do you want to eat cake, or rice?
5. He wants to learn Baba Malay, because he is Peranakan.

Answers: 1. Lu mia hia, ato/ka lu mia tachi mo datang. 2. Ben mo bawak kereta, tapi dia tak'ah kereta. 3. Gua mo pi Australia, pasair gua mo tengok kangaroos. 4. Lu mo makan kueh, ato nasi? 5. Dia mo belajair Chakapan Baba, pasair dia orang Peranakan.

Translate into English

1. Gua mo pi Australia, pasair gua mo tengok koala.
2. Lu mo pi kebun, ato sana?
3. Jorang mo beli barang, tapi jorang tak'ah duit.
4. Lu mo hia, ato tachi mo datang?
5. Lu orang tak mo pi sekolah, pasair lu orang tak mo belajair.

Answers: 1. I want to go to Australia, because I want to see koalas. 2. Do you want to go to the garden, or there? 3. They want to buy things, but they have no money. 4. Is your big brother, or big sister coming? 5. You all don't want to go to school, because you all don't want to study.

All of you must learn Baba Malay.

KALU - If

Dog = Anjing

Kalu = If
As a conjunction, **IF** is used to say that B will happen **IF** A happens.

KALU, lu tak makan, lu mesti mati.
IF, you don't eat, you will die.

Kalu, lu tak mo kerja, lu tak boleh dapat duit.
If, you don't work, you won't get money.

IF, can also show if a thing is true.

Kalu, jorang pi Australia, jorang boleh tengok kangaroo.
If, they go to Australia, they can see kangaroos.

IF, can also be used to make a request.

Kalu, dia pi Australia, gua kasi dia tengok koala.
If, he goes to Australia, I will let him see a koala.

Glossary
Dapat = Get
Duit = Money
Jorang = They
Kasi = Give or Let
Tengok = See
Mati = Die   Mesti = Must, Will

Kita mo belajair Baba Malay.

SUNGGUPUN - Although

Irene

Sunggupun = Although
As a conjunction, **ALTHOUGH** is used to say that despite something being the case, something else will happen.

SUNGGUPUN, Irene makan manyak, dia lagik lapair sair.
ALTHOUGH, Irene ate a lot, she is still hungry.

Sunggupun, saya pi keday, saya tak beli barang.
Although, I went to the shop, I didn't buy anything.

Sunggupun, dia bikin exercise, dia lagik gemok.
Although, he exercises, he is still fat.

> Glossary
> Gemok = Fat
> Lagik = Still
> Lapair = Hungry
> Keday = Shop/s
> Manyak = A lot
> Masih = Still
> Sair = From Sekali meaning indeed or truly
> Sekali = From Kali meaning times i.e. an occasion; an instance (Sekali has more than one meaning.)

CHOBAK - KALU/SUNGGUPUN

Car = Kereta

Select the correct word

1. Although, your big sister can drive, she doesn't have a car.
   (Kalu/Sunggupun), lu mia tachi boleh bawak kereta, dia tak'ah kereta.

2. If, your big sister can drive, she must buy a car.
   (Kalu/Sunggupun), lu mia tachi boleh bawak kereta, dia mesti beli kereta.

3. If, you buy a car, you must learn to drive.
   (Kalu/Sunggupun), lu beli kereta, lu mesti belajair bawak kereta.

4. Although, you bought a car, you cannot drive.
   (Kalu/Sunggupun), lu beli kereta, lu tak boleh bawak kereta.

5. Although, he bought a car, he doesn't drive.
   (Kalu/Sunggupun), dia beli kereta, dia tak boleh bawak kereta.

Answers: 1. Sunggupun. 2. Kalu. 3. Kalu. 4. Sunggupun. 5. Sunggupun.

Glossary
Boleh = Can
Tak Boleh = Cannot

CHOBAK - TAPI/KA/PASAIR/KALU/SUNGGUPUN

Things = Barang

Translate into English

1. Ni bukan bunga, tapi pokok.

2. Sunggupun, gua tak'ah duit, gua suka beli barang.

3. Gua boleh beli nasi, ka kueh.

4. Kalu, lu beli nasi, lu boleh makan.

5. Gua beli nasi, pasair gua mo makan.

6. Kalu gua beli nasi, gua boleh makan, tapi tak'ah nasi beli.

7. Beli nasi ka kueh, pasair gua mo makan.

Answers: 1. This is not a flower, but a tree. 2. Although I have no money, I like buying things. 3. I can buy rice or cake. 4. If, you buy rice, you can eat. 5. I bought rice, because I want to eat. 6. If I bought rice, I can eat, but there is no rice to buy. 7. Buy rice or cake, because I want to eat.

SAMA - With

Work = Kerja

With = Sama

The word '**SAMA**' is the closest thing that Baba Malay has to the conjunction '**AND**'. However, it is used more as '**WITH**' or '**SAME**' or '**TOGETHER**'.

    Sentence 1:   Ben kerja kat sana.
                           Ben works there.

    Sentence 2:   Irene kerja kat sana.
                           Irene works there.

    Joined: Ben **SAMA** Irene kerja kat sana.
                         Ben **SAME WITH** Irene works there.
                         Ben **TOGETHER WITH** Irene works there.

So how do we use **AND** in BABA MALAY?

In English we would say, "I bought milk, rice and bread."
In Baba Malay we say, "Gua beli susu, nasi, roti."

The conjunction **AND** (used to join words, phrases etc. together) is inferred.

Sometimes however, the Malay word '**DAN**' is used as in, "Gua beli susu, nasi, **DAN** roti."

PASAIR TU - So

Money = Duit

So, Because of that = Pasair Tu

In Baba Malay, the word '**SO**' functions a lot like '**BECAUSE**' by providing a reason.

Sentence 1:   Gua mia adek jantan mo makan.
              My younger brother wants to eat.

Sentence 2:   Gua mia adek jantan masak.
              My younger brother cooks.

Joined: Gua mia adek jantan mo makan, **PASAIR TU** gua mia adek jantan masak.
              My younger brother wants to eat, **SO** my younger brother cooks.

Example: Gua mia adek prompuan mo duit, **PASAIR TU** dia kerja. My younger sister wants money, **SO BECAUSE OF THAT** she works.

Glossary

Adek Jantan = Younger Brother
Adek Prompuan = Younger Sister
Masak = Cook

ABIS - So, Then, Therefore, In the End

Office/Place of Work = Tempat Kerja

So, then, therefore, in the end = Abis

From the word '**HABIS**' which means finished. Also, used as the conjunction '**SO**'. Synonymous with '**PASAIR TU**'. But it is when '**ABIS**' is used as '**THEN**', meaning 'next' that it comes into its own.

Example (Used as **SO**): Gua mia adek prompuan mo belajair Chakapan Baba, **ABIS** dia beli buku.
My younger sister wants to learn Baba Malay, **SO** she bought a book.

Example (Used as **THEN**): **ABIS,** gua mia adek jantan pi tempat kerja.
THEN, my younger brother went to the office.

Example (Used as **THEREFORE**): **ABIS**, gua mia adek jantan makan kueh, pasair dia lapair.
IN THE END, my younger brother ate the cake, because he was hungry.

Glossary

Adek Jantan = Younger Brother
Adek Prompuan = Younger Sister
Belajair = Learn/Study
Lapair = Hungry

CHOBAK - SAMA/PASAIR TU/ABIS/DAN

Rice = Nasik

Select the correct word

1. My little sister, with my little brother eat cake.
   Gua mia adek prompuan, (sama/pasair tu/abis/dan) gua mia adek jantan eat cake.

2. So, your big sister can drive.
   (Sama/Pasair Tu/Abis/Dan), lu mia tachi boleh bawak kereta.

3. So, I bought a book and then I studied.
   (Sama/Pasair Tu/Abis/Dan), gua beli buku, (sama/abis/dan) gua belajair.

4. In the end, they went to work.
   (Sama/Abis/Dan), jorang pi kerja.

5. My big brother, and my big sister did not eat rice, so they could eat cake.
   Gua mia hia, (sama/pasair tu/abis/dan) gua mia tachi tak makan nasi, (sama/pasair tu/abis/dan) makan kueh.

Answers: 1. Sama. 2. Pasair tu or Abis. 3. Pasair tu or Abis, abis.
4. Abis. 5. Sama or Dan. pasair tu or abis.

Forms of Conjunctions in English

After — Lepair
As — Macham
Although — Sunggupun
And — Technically there is no 'and' in Baba, but sometimes the Malay word 'dan' is used. Or 'sama'.
Because — Pasair/Sebab/Kerna
Before — Depan/Sebelum/Dulu
But — Tapi
For — Buat (preposition)
If — Kalu
Nor — Technically no Nor
Now — Sekarang/Ni jam
Once — Sekali (See Page 19)
Or — Ka or Ato
Since — Sejak, lagik tadik, lagikan
So — Pasair tu or Abis
Then — Abis (Sometimes interchanged with Pasair Tu)
Therefore — Abis
Until — Sampay
When — Bila
Whenever — Bila-bila
While — Technically there is no exact term for this
With — Sama
Yet — Belom lagik

(Note: Some words function as conjunctions as well as prepositions or adverbs etc. depending on the context.)

Gua nanti chuchi pinggan-mangkok, lepair jorang balek.
I'll wash the plates and bowls, after they leave. Or I'll wash up, after they leave.

Dia kaya macham dia mia hia.
He's as rich as his brother.

Gua sama gua mia kawan jalan pelan-pelan.
I with my friend walk slowly.

Gua makan ayam, babi, kambeng.
I eat chicken, pork and lamb.

Gua makan ayam, babi, sama kambeng.
I eat chicken, pork and lamb.

Gua makan ayam, babi, dan kambeng.
I eat chicken, pork and lamb.

Gua mo pi pantai, pasair gua mo berenang.
I want to go to the beach, because I want to swim.

Lu mo makan, sebab lu lapair.
You want to eat, because you are hungry.

Kita mo chakap Baba, kerna kita mo belajair Chakapan Baba.
We must speak Baba, because we want to learn Baba Malay.

Depan gua pi kerja, gua mesti belajair.
Before I go to work, I must study.

Sebelum gua pi kerja, gua mesti belajair.
Before I go to work, I must study.

Dulu gua pi kerja, gua mesti belajair.
Before I go to work, I must study.

Lu mo pi cinema, tapi lu tak'ah duit.
You want to go to the cinema, but you have no money.

Gua beli ni buat makan malam.
I bought this for dinner.

Kalu saya tak kerja, saya tak'ah duit.
If I do not work, I have no money.

Sekarang, saya mo makan kueh.
Now, I want to eat cake.

Ni jam saya mo makan nasi.
Now I want to eat rice.

Sekali, saya pi New Zealand. Dua kali, saya pi Fiji.
Once, I went to New Zealand. Twice, I went to Fiji.

Gua makan ayam ato kambing.
I will eat chicken or goat.

Gua makan ayam ka kambing.
I will eat chicken or goat.

Sejak belajair Chakapan Baba, saya mesti chakap manyak.
Since learning Baba Malay, I must speak a lot.

Lagik tadik belajair Chakapan Baba, gua mesti chakap manyak.
Since learning Baba Malay, I must speak a lot.

Lagikan belajair Chakapan Baba, gua mesti chakap manyak.
Since learning Baba Malay, I must speak a lot.

Saya pi kebun, pasair tu saya boleh tengok bunga.
I go to the garden, so I can see the flowers.

Saya pi kebun, abis saya boleh tengok bunga.
I go to the garden, then/so I can see the flowers.

Saya mo chakap Chakapan Baba, abis saya mo belajair Chakapan Baba.
I want to speak Baba Malay, therefore I must learn Baba Malay.

Saya makan, sampay kenyang.
I eat, until I am full.

Bila–bila saya pi Singapore, saya makan manyak laok embok-embok.
Whenever I go to Singapore, I eat a lot of Peranakan food.

Saya tak pi Italy belom-lagik.
I have not been to Italy yet.

Glossary
Ayam = Chicken
Babi = Pork
Berenang = Swim
Belajair = Learn
Boleh = Can
Bunga = Flower or flowers depending on the context
Chakap = Speak, Chakapan = Language
Duit = Money
Kambing/Kambeng = Mutton/Goat
Kaya = Rich
Kawan = Friend
Lapair = Hungry
Laok Embok-embok = Peranakan Food
Makan Malam = Dinner
Manyak = Plenty or a lot
Pantai = Beach
Pelan-pelan = Slowly
Pinggan-mangkok = Plates and bowls i.e., crockery
Tengok = See

NOTES

Baba Malay or Chakapan Baba or the Baba language was born when Chinese traders sailed down to Southeast Asia and intermarried with the local women. A mix of Hokkien and Malay, Baba Malay went into decline after WWII as many Peranakans were killed.

This is the reason why there are no Baba Malay equivalent to some words today. When in doubt English words are often used.

Another reason is language assimilation.

There are also two registers to Baba Malay:

1. Alus i.e., a refined form that women tended to speak.
2. Kasair i.e., a coarser version practised by men.

Baba Malay tended to be spoken rather than written so there are many variations in the spelling e.g.,

kreja or kerja (work)

When in doubt I referred to Kenneth Chan's *Baba Malay For Everyone - A comprehensive guide to the Peranakan language* as well as William Gwee Thian Hock's *A Baba Malay Dictionary.*

Baba Malay is also sadly considered an endangered language.

Let's do our best to change this!

Bibek Theresa

About the Author

Theresa Fuller

Theresa Fuller has always loved stories and story-telling, but it was not until the birth of her first son that she became a full-time writer. Her aim was to write stories about her culture: Southeast Asia.

Theresa was Head of Computing at various private schools in Sydney. She has also been a Higher School Certificate (HSC) Examiner and HSC Assessor. Her teaching degrees have seen her work in primary and secondary schools and at Kalgoorlie College in Western Australia.

Her first published novel in 2018 was *THE GHOST ENGINE*, a steampunk fantasy about the fictitious granddaughter of Ada Lovelace, the world's first programmer. Theresa has published books on Southeast Asian mythology: *THE GIRL WHO BECAME A GODDESS* (2019), *THE GIRL SUDAN PAINTED LIKE A GOLD RING* (2022) and *EATING THE LIVER OF THE EARTH* - collection of the lost folktales of the mousedeer Sang Kanchel.

In 2023, *WHERE CRANES WEAVE AND BAMBOO SINGS* a visual narrative textbook for children and beginner writers was published.

In 2020, Theresa lost many family members. She threw heself into researching her family history as a way to deal with her grief. This was when she discovered that the language of her ancestors - Baba Malay - was on the verge of extinction. As a writer, teacher and selfpublishing author, Theresa found herself in an unusual position - she was able to create the curriculum that was needed to help fill a vacuum.

The result is the **Baba Malay Today** series. And now the **New Peranakan Tales** series starting with GUA PI KEDAY.

All in aid of saving the language.

www.theresafuller.com

Thank you for your support!

More Books in the Baba Malay Today Series

Book 1 - Interrogatory Part I   SAPA, APA, MANA or
WHO, WHAT, WHERE

Book 2 - Interrogatory Part II   AMCHAM, APASAIR, BILA or
HOW, WHY, WHEN

Book 3 - Conjunctions   TAPI, ABIS, PASAIR or
BUT, SO, BECAUSE

Book 4 - Prepositions   ATAIR, KAT, BAWAH or
TOP, NEAR, BOTTOM

Book 5 - Antonyms   ALUS, KA, KASAR or
DELICATE, OR, COARSE

Book 6 - Essence   CHAKAPAN BABA ATI or
THE HEART OF BABA MALAY

Book 7 - Poetry   CHAKAPAN BABA PANTON or
BABA MALAY POETRY

Book 8 - Idioms   CHAKAPAN BABA CHAKAPAN or
BABA MALAY IDIOMS

Dear Reader,

Thank you for the purchase of this book.

Please help us spread the word as we try to save our language.

Bibek Theresa

Sydney, 18th of June, 2022

Jangan lupa Chakapan Baba.